Leap

Claire Bateman

New Issues Poetry & Prose

A Green Rose Book

New Issues Poetry & Prose
The College of Arts and Sciences
Western Michigan University
Kalamazoo, Michigan 49008

First Edition, 2005.

ISBN   1-930974-55-8 (paperbound)

Library of Congress Cataloging-in-Publication Data:
Bateman, Claire
Leap/Claire Bateman
Library of Congress Control Number: 2005922613

Editor   Herbert Scott
Copy Editor   Lisa Lishman
Managing Editor   Marianne Swierenga
Designer   Carl Bean-Larson
Art Director   Tricia Hennessy
Production Manager   Paul Sizer
                              The Design Center, Department of Art
                              College of Fine Arts
                              Western Michigan University

Leap

Claire Bateman

Claire Bateman

New Issues

 WESTERN MICHIGAN UNIVERSITY

Also by Claire Bateman

to Matt Bateman & Jon Bateman

Contents

I.

Garb

To shop is to seek out one of the soul's external aspects, the object being not discovery but recognition.

To believe in such a reunion is not, however, to infer a prior incompleteness. Socrates, though not himself a shopper, made quite a point of this.

Daphne did not have access to a mirror when her skin first crusted over with the silvery bark, her hair twisted into leaf & shadow. You could say she was shopping in something of a hurry.

First thought: best thought, she murmurs to herself each spring.

The opposite of any garment is neither flesh nor emptiness.

While my mother browsed the stocked racks at Lord & Taylor, I sat amidst fallen apparel, pricking out names for myself with straight pins on the heavy carpet that bore me up & carried me through layers of solitude, each more illumined than the last.

Floor, this is your dress.
Dress, this is your floor.

Landlocked

Swaying together on their Topeka clothesline like synchronized swimmers, the dresses yet again sense the water abandoning their fibers for the sky. Though they experience evaporation every Monday afternoon, they are no less petulant today than they were the very first time they were clipped up with wooden pins to dry. If only they might *remain* wet, they could continue to pretend that they are the dresses of drowning victims, a status to which they all aspire: the spreading, the billowing, the floating, & then the saturation, the heaviness, the delicious sinking. Clearly, the Pre-Raphaelite sensibilities of these dresses doom them to permanent neurosis—is this an aesthetic or a moral flaw? Either way, it is incurable. Hours of psychotherapeutic intervention might modify their craving, so that they would, perhaps, be content to become baptismal gowns, but nothing could displace their obsession with going under.

"The Top 21 Holiday, Party, & Everyday Stains, & How to Remove Them"

Predictably, correction fluid & crayons
have made the list, but what about
spinach & turnip blood—
why are they not included?
Eggnog, lipstick, & even (as if to mock!)
Silly Putty are present & accounted for,
but what about gunpowder, red clay, & cement dust,
not to mention magma, lava, & ash—
did anyone think to consult
the former residents of Pompeii,
or, in the composition of such rosters,
are the dead, by definition, ostracized?
What about pitch, what about tar,
what about high voltage scorchings & singeings?
And the tree that falls in a forest where no one hears—
does it not leave a singular stain
of suffering & birdsong?
What about white sheets
trailing from the mattress onto a white carpet;
what about frost light & eel light;
the melody that declines to resolve
into the tonic—
without treatment,
do not these also
threaten to become
indelible?

Leap

Consider the formal requirements of the braid.

The hair must be imagined as not only non-unitary, but tripartite as well;

the strands must be pre-visualized as twisted & interlaced: over, under, around, between, in an unbroken pattern;

the problem of securing the tip must be foreseen & overcome by conceptualizing a flexible filament that loops around itself.

To conceive of all of this, one must have already mastered the theories of unravelling & release; binding & protection; predestination & free will; wave action; narrative resolution, & the rupture of the trance state.

The distance between absolute braidlessness & the first braid was astronomical compared to the scarcely noticeable gap between the simple braid & the double braid; the herringbone braid; the warhorse's mane plaited with tiny bells; braided tiaras with feathers & floating tourmalines; cornrows; ply-splitting; brocading; the bobbin; the shuttle; the cotton gin; Bob Marley; the polynomial; DNA; modal jazz harmonics; & the thirteen simultaneous plotlines of *General Hospital*.

Domesticity

The dollhouse was so exquisite that the servants, finding it uncanny, refused to approach it, so the little girl understood that she must dust it herself. And dust it she did, with the regular feather duster for the roof & exterior walls, & the dollhouse-size feather duster for the billiard table, the sideboards, the tea wagon, the bassinet, the four-posters, the chiffonier, the escritoire, the overflowing coal scuttle, the eggcups, the shaving brush, the boar's head forever on the verge of utterance, the little man with his spreading sideburns, his widow's peak, & his historical sense of injury, & the little woman with her diamond teardrop earrings & secret Swedenborgian leanings. Also the baby, whose wax was still soft & warm, & the little dollhouse girl, who had lost her pearl ring in her long golden hair where it ceaselessly traveled, in love with its private itinerary.

Clasps

Of all inanimate entities, jewelry clasps are by far the most treacherous. The hook & eye, the toggle, the spring ring, the hinged foldover fastener—no matter how guileless they appear amidst their floral or filigreed settings, you must never let down your guard in their presence. Predominant in their nature is the natural viciousness of any creature with whom everyone else is at a permanent disadvantage. The necklace clasp we must struggle with blindly, our hair tangled & wrenched by its tiny, perfect incisors, the bracelet clasp we must attempt to subdue with our inept, non-dominant hand. Oh, there are chokers who decline for hours to fasten at all, & then, at bedtime, refuse to come off. There are heirloom lockets whose clasps close sweetly; later that day, you sense an alarming lightness, & discover their permanent, heart-shaped absence. It's true, of course, that a few freakish adornments put up no resistance to being donned or removed, but these the other jewels torment cruelly in the sinister darkness of the lacquered box. Don't trust them: like heretics or fifth columnists, they could, at any moment, turn.

Dumpster Couch

Upended by the dumpster, the old sofa fears that the garbage truck might arrive before the rain.

According to passersby, the prediction is for light showers, or at least drizzle, within the next twenty-four hours, but the sofa isn't holding its breath. It's spent thirty-six seasons—nearly a lifetime in upholstery years—basking in the radiance of the Failed Weather Channel where impeccably dressed anchorpersons stride back & forth in front of an illuminated map portraying weather patterns that did not develop as the meteorologists had anticipated.

The people with whom the sofa has spent its life are Failed Weather Channel junkies. Not only do they wake & sleep to its theme music, but they even keep track of the anchorpeople's hairstyles & wardrobes. Thus, the sofa is well-acquainted with all the phenomena of failed weather: the windows boarded up against the hurricane that at the last moment veers unexpectedly out to sea; the bride's languorously-blossoming bruises acquired during the freak hailstorm that arrives like a violent uninvited guest at the garden wedding reception.

The sofa can actually feel the absence of rain wrapping itself around it like an eiderdown which, if wishes were needles, would by now be punctured by a million wounds for the needle-like drops to enter, creating pore-like openings in the fabric through which the flock of miniature doves the sofa is stuffed with would at last be released to ascend.

Sweet

Goldilocks finds the cottage oddly familiar,
even to the rich, ripe scent of childhood—whose?
The big bed is like a giant custard;
it loves her too greedily.
The middle bed is prim as a porcelain pillbox;
it has everything to do with reform,
& nothing with comfort.
The little bed is just lonely enough to please her.
Tucked in by her imaginary nanny,
she's a compact sugar bomb.
The whole cottage fears her kamakazi heart,
standard in quiescent little girls;
the hearth tongs tiptoe out in the company of the teapot
as everything dismantles itself around her
until the clipped lawn, strewn with domestic items,
resembles a flea market in fugue state.

Meanwhile, deep in the woods,
the Bears are taking their walk.
Their clothes make them a little anxious:
starched ruffles & buttons—
also, walking upright.
Baby Bear murmurs a slight song:
We are harmless, harmless.
Is this what bears do? they wonder,
not actually knowing
any other bears.

Sisters

The moment the door of Mother's taxi slammed, leaving Myra Louise in charge for the week, she announced that because she detested vacuuming & despised the odors of ammonia & wax, we were forbidden to set foot on any of the floors. Thus, it was by the power of her ferocity alone that we floated scufflessly several inches over the carpets & tiles for the entire duration of Mother's absence. When we began to feel nauseous from lack of contact with solid ground, we were instructed to go outside & stand on the sidewalk, not the grass, which was to remain unruffled.

Myra Louise didn't like to make beds, either, so we were commanded to hover over the top quilt. When we grew chilly in the small hours of the morning, we were allowed to put on our coats, but we were not permitted to come within an arm's-length distance of the bed. I remember noticing that plump little Angela in her brown mackinaw resembled a short thick wiener being turned on a spit as she rotated slowly, but apparently not uncomfortably, in the air above her cot while Myra Louise shone her ubiquitous flashlight around the room to make sure that no one was illicitly touching down.

The Pale Dress

Left for dead in an alley, the dress was rescued by the Sisters of Mercy, who laid it on a bed of sweet medicinal oils in the company of other dresses reclining together in various stages of recovery.

After the second week, Sister Punctillia, the new infirmarian, requested permission to discontinue treatment. "Look at her," she said. "She's ghastly. If she were going to get better, she would have begun to do so by now. The vocation of our order is to minister to the sick, not to raise the dead!"

But Mother Hannah of the Multiplying Sorrows shook her head. "I've known legions of dresses in my lifetime," she said. "I've seen ball gowns & back wraps, muu-muus & dirndls. I've seen tennis dresses & A-lines, pinafores & jumpers. I've seen them rise up cured after twelve hours of bed rest, & be released to the streets, only to stagger in through that door in tatters the very next day. Never trust a fast-healing dress; it's bound to be unstable. But a slow-healing dress is a quality dress. Just wait & see."

Come spring, however, the dress was still pallid & weak. Other dresses had come & gone, but this dress seemed unable to even turn over on her own, let alone get out of bed. Again Sister Punctillia challenged the Superior. "Mother," she said, "I know a shirker when I meet one. This dress simply doesn't want to fend for herself. I say we give her a swift boot in the rear, & send her out the door."

"See how pale she continues to be," clucked Mother Hannah. "That kind of anemia can't be faked."

"Maybe she's albino," Sister Punctillia said. "Maybe she's Nordic—maybe she's even *Lutheran!*"

"Nonsense," the Mother retorted.

But after the second winter, she too became concerned, thinking guiltily of the many invalids she'd had to turn away for the sake of the pale dress. And she was not unaware of the fact that Sister Punctillia was attempting to stir up mutiny within the ranks of the newest sisters.

So Mother Hannah retired to her cell to meditate & study. After several days, she emerged, gathered the community, & announced, "I have reviewed every page in the Book of Earthly Dresses, & the pale dress does not appear on any of them. I therefore suspect that she is the long-prophesied Visitation Dress who has come to earth to assess the worthiness of our order. I believe that by taking her in from the street, we have passed the first test, which was, no doubt, for hospitality, & by keeping her all this time, we have passed the second, which must have been for longsuffering."

The members of the order trembled. "What is the nature of the third test?" one of them quavered.

"I think," sighed Mother Hannah, "that we must discover the way to make her bloom."

So they brought the dress out to the convent garden & released swarms of honeybees in her presence, & they bore her on a milk-white mare into a meadow full of fragrance & clover light, & they draped her over the perpetually pellucid brooklet that was permanently short of breath because it couldn't stop chuckling, but the dress remained droopy & gray. Then they soaked her in champagne for three days & three nights, & they flew her from a string like a kite, & they warmed her on "low" in the oven, but her hue, or lack thereof, was still unchanged.

Some of the nuns grew despondent, & others became cynical, speculating that this was not the Visitation Dress at all, but merely an ordinary masochist dress in disguise, the kind that had become so warped in parochial school that she was permanently fixated on return. "Let's drown her," they hissed. "Let's incinerate her. Let's smear her with rabbit blood & offer her to the convent wolves for a treat. Isn't that just what she's been begging for?"

So they drugged Mother Hannah's tea with sleeping potion, & while she was unconscious on her hard, narrow bed, they absconded with the dress, taking her first to the town pond, where, though swiftly & verifiably waterlogged, she remained serenely on the surface, skirt outspread like an oversized water lily, & then to the incinerator, where she took on not even the slightest singe mark. By this point, they dared not give her to the wolves. So they placed her on her infirmary bed, where she lay exactly as she had all this time, as though nothing had ever happened.

A soberness of spirit descended upon the sisterhood. Some of them began to avoid the infirmary at all costs, busying themselves with other community duties that would keep them as distant as possible from the mysterious dress. Others, who insisted upon keeping perpetual vigil around the cot on which the dress repined, eventually fainted or became ill with exhaustion, & had to be forcibly removed because the crowding was creating a fire hazard. Sister Punctillia became the most devoted of all, chaining herself to the leg of the dress's cot & swallowing the padlock key so that no one could take her away. Because the dress's presence was threatening the order's internal stability as well as its mission on behalf of damaged & languishing dresses everywhere, Mother Hannah took drastic measures. After separating Sister Punctillia from her chains by means of an electric saw, she isolated the dress in a little cubicle of its own, which she then bricked in by hand, declaring that it must never be spoken of again. But she was too late. The order disintegrated anyway, since the dress's absence obsessed the sisters even more than had its presence, & because they neglected their ministry, the townspeople withdrew their support & evicted the nuns.

The sisters wandered off toward the forest & surrounding roads, some in small groups, & some alone, followed by the convent wolves & the few limping gowns who had been their final patients. Inside its brick sarcophagus within the convent walls, the pale dress began to glow, having at last been granted the gift of absolute darkness.

Climatology

When the dads woke up from their naps,
the sides of their faces were cross-hatched
with sofa weave, as if they'd been couch-men,
like centaurs, freshly split.

When the dads woke up from their naps,
the insides of their mouths stank,
but their bellies were filled with sweetness.

When the dads woke up from their naps,
their white undershirts were thin with wear,
tender as a toddler's blanket.

When the dads woke up from their naps,
it was suddenly twilight;
if the word "crepuscular" had not already been available,
the dads would have had to convene in order to invent it,
along with Impressionism,
the idea of mauve,
& the history of melancholy.

When the dads woke up from their naps,
it was apparent that Mister Sun was at last the victor
in his long tug-of-war with the upholstery,
having sucked back into his surface
the living room's goldenrod, its sepia,
& even the eggshell ecru of the dust ruffles,
so everything now appeared blanched
though uncomplaining.

When the dads woke up from their naps,
each found himself alone in his house
with only the sound of the air conditioner
grinding August to the bone.

Where was everyone?

The dads took a few centuries to ponder this question
while they scratched the backs of their necks.
Comets sped across the sky
in pursuit of one another,
the continental shelf shrugged in & out of position,
& tectonic plates shifted
lightly in their sleep.

After a while, each dad
wandered to his front door,
which, contrary to explicit instructions,
had been left open,
air conditioning the whole outdoors.
The yards were a single frozen tundra,
the fences long-since blown down,
the mail boxes stove in,
& the asphalt of the street
was covered with ice
across which a Kodiak bear shambled,
slow as a drowsy dad.

Insomniac

You curse your list, but it is love
that keeps you awake,
the world indigestible inside you—
fact, contingency,
everything that depends on you
for its rough passage.
You are its involution of space,
its deep & traveling
darkness of God,
desired, not known.
It is your work to hold
all things uncomfortably
intact in your belly,
so that blue & violet
do not melt & run together;
so that the creeping moss
does not blend into the oak;
so that your neighbor who dislikes you
does not waver in his task.

But you are only
a late arrival, human.
In you there is something
that would sink back
into its first dream,
& the world, dissolving,
would give itself up,
indistinguishable
from yourself.

In the severe jewel-light
of your bedside clock,
you rightly toss & turn
against that rest.

Therapeutic

Frowning, the doctor prescribes mandatory complete bed rest for an unspecified length of time.

Now beds everywhere must be stripped & dismantled.

Now all the mattresses in the world must be laid gently end-to-end around the globe to rock in Baltic brine or adorn the ice-lacquered Alps.

Now the parking lots & soccer fields of the nations must become a vast, non-contiguous dormitory of drowsy bedsprings no longer forced to chatter in their sleep.

That clatter of boots on the stairway, that heavy midnight knock shuddering against your door: the police have arrived to investigate rumors of illegal possession.

It's that moldy, rolled-up hammock in your basement—but of all your neighbors & loved ones, who was it that turned you in?

Trauma Treatment

I'm the one whom objects seek out, trembling, after the telemetrist gets through with them. The blanched glove, the hysterical set of keys, the shoe with its tongue hanging out, twitching: I don't know how they locate me, how they manage the pilgrimage, but everywhere I go, they appear in my path. You see, not only do they wish to keep their secrets from others, but they possess an innate resistance to remembering their own histories, which is why the telemetrist's accomplishment represents such a deep violation of their very essence.

The treatment is simple, & you should know it, just as you should understand the basics of CPR. First, cover your hand with a towel to protect the object from the sensation of human touch, which it now associates with degradation. Then, hold the object in your palm & address it in a low voice, according to its particular frequency—you'll have to practice becoming nearly inaudible. Murmur to it of buried things: the golden combs Noah's daughters left behind, now safe under miles of silt; a ship's captain's reading glasses secure in a thicket of anemones on the Pacific floor; glossy Bi-Lo coupons curled tightly at the heart of a landfill. Speak to it of avalanches, of sedimentary rock, of the languorous settling of soils. Then place it gently in your freezer, where the cold will slow its vibrations even further. There it will begin to forget everything it's revealed, & eventually, everything it knows.

After a full year, you may remove it, & let it sit mutely in your bare hand, wholly restored to the impersonal, ready to be released into the world. But if by chance the object is still unhealed, as is occasionally the case, you must transfer it to a dark place in your home where it will never be disturbed. If you're the sort of housekeeper who regularly cleans & airs all your cupboards & drawers, & thus have no place for such an invalid, then, with it wrapped in a dishcloth like a broken-winged robin fledgling, approach one of your less fastidious neighbors, & beg him to take it in, which he will probably do, though not out of any love for you, who have been snubbing him all these years.

Service

I find that somehow, I've acquired cable service for which I've never paid. Thus, I have access to the Anesthesia Channel, the Lost-&-Missing Channel, the Phantom Sobriety Channel, the Sargasso Sea Channel, & many others whose theme songs I've yet to memorize. My favorite is the Woodstove Channel, such a low-budget operation that usually, all I can glimpse is a bed of coals glowing, warm but not too bright.

FAQ's About Invisible Fence, Inc.

1. *What is the installation procedure for Invisible Fence?*

Two licensed professionals will perform the installation work. Their names are Ronnie & J.T., & you will be made aware of their arrival by the beeping sound of the invisible truck backing into your driveway. Invisible Fence, Inc. retains no liability for tricycles, garden hoses, or other items flattened or in any way damaged by said truck. The actual installation, which will take less than an hour, involves sophisticated radioactive & electromagnetic equipment; please do not distract our professionals by speaking to them or attempting to locate them by swinging a stick around in the vicinity of their footprints or voices. Also, because by the end of the process they will be suffering from dehydration resulting from excessive perspiration due to the intensity of their concentration & the delicacy of their fine motor work, please be sure that you have left cold drinks for them under a shady tree. Ronnie likes sweet tea prepared with jasmine, rosehips, frozen uncut strawberries, & perfectly spherical miniature ice cubes that chime like the bells his grandmother suspended over his crib; J.T., who aspires to the pirate life, prefers dark-roasted, full-bodied Guatemalan-blend iced coffee with a trace of chicory & a generous slosh of golden Bacardi.

2. *Might Invisible Fence prove harmful to my pet(s) or to humans in its vicinity, such as family members or visitors?*

Anyone who asks this sort of question needs to get him or herself down to Home Depot & purchase the materials for a perceptible fence. A manifest fence. A flagrant fence.

3. *What have customers said about Invisible Fence?*

"After the very first time my Sookie hurled her little body against Invisible Fence & felt herself disappearing, she never attempted to escape again."—Mrs. Myra Jane Abney, Gusto Falls, Idaho

"We tried some of the cheaper competition brands first, even experimented with the so-called 'easy-install-it-yourself' kind, but as the saying goes, you get what you pay for. The cheap brands lost the crisp cleanness of their invisibility within weeks, so we were stuck with a sloppy fog we had to pay someone to remove. And as for the self-install kind—'easy'—ha! My husband is still missing the tip of his thumb, but parts of the fence were plain as day by the second morning. We found out the hard way that nothing beats Invisible Fence for convenience & reliability."—Mrs. Abby Franck, Salt Lake City, Utah

4. What other services are available through your organization?

We are a subsidiary of Invisible Obstructions, International, which is fully equipped to meet all your obstacle needs, supplying invisible speed bumps, roadblocks, bulkheads, dikes, logjams, & hydraulic dams to residences, businesses, & every level of government worldwide. And be on the lookout for the fine work that will soon be available from our brand new Psyops Division, which will provide a wide variety of one hundred percent covert denials, obfuscations, resistances, repressions, & mental blocks.

Phone Apology

I'm sorry I'm not Maria. I'm sorry I can't speak Spanish so that I could explain this to you. I did take three years of French in high school, but the only complete sentence I can remember is: *Regarde comme elle tombe, cette belle neige,* which, translated literally, means, *Watch how she falls, the beautiful snow,* useless in this situation, since it's neither your language nor mine, & because it isn't snow you seek, but Maria. Whoever she is, I hope you find her soon, though with each phone call you sound so increasingly anxious, I think that this number, which happens to continually & relentlessly not be hers, is the only means you have of trying to reach her. I'm sorry that on your fourth attempt, I made the mistake of saying, *There is no Maria here,* since I could tell by your immediate waterfall of exclamation that you mistook my use of her name for an acknowledgement that she was currently present, or had been, or would be soon. In actual fact, however, there is not even one Maria in my life. If there were, I would ask her to come over & answer the phone, no matter which languages she knew or did not know. It makes me sad on your behalf that there are so many combinations of numbers in this world. It makes me sad that the only one that can connect you to Maria is not the one you have been dialing. I wish I could retroactively grant myself some other number, some whole other telephone history, so that this *could* be hers—unless, of course, she made up this number on purpose so that you would be sure to not find her, which might be an even sadder story than the one in which you've gotten her number wrong. Or maybe they're equally sad, love being no less cruel than numbers in any speech.

The Free Zone

While reading, you are not idling, lazing, loitering, dilly-dallying, or procrastinating. In fact, time spent reading is not even deducted from your lifespan. When your nose is, as some so pejoratively put it, "stuck in a book," you do not actually age. If Ponce de Leon had been aware of this, he wouldn't have gone searching for the Fountain of Youth in, of all places, Florida, & would thus have spared himself that fatal trip through the swampland with its malign efflorescence, its smoldering stagnation & decay which induced in him a trance broken only by the grunting & squealing of feral pigs crashing through the underbrush. Such is the life of the man of action who shuns the silence & solitude of the printed page—though it's sad, it does give us something to read about.

Babyhood

That state of simultaneous humiliation & decadence from which full recovery is not possible.

Such a dubious condition that even its pairs of adjectives fail to correlate. "Easy baby" is to "good baby" as "difficult baby" is to–what? "Evil baby"? But as if by definition, there are no evil babies, except for Richard II, who according to legend sulked in his mother's womb for two years, & was, upon emerging, already fully equipped with hair, teeth, & a brutal temper.

People you have found to be otherwise trustworthy claim it's you in the old photo, permanently lashed into a wooden high chair, glaring at the spoon. One must forever maintain with that Ur-self the most unnatural, the most queasy, the most compromised of relationships, characterized by more embarrassment, bewilderment, remorse, & historical affection than one's relationship with any other individual.

Behold, there passeth yet another baby with its entourage of equipment-bearing caretakers, a scene whose clamor & clutter exceeds that of any in *Ben-Hur*.

Trailing clouds of glory, murmured William Wordsworth in rapture, having long since abandoned his own baby. Trailing placentas, trailing fever dreams, trailing ships weighed down nearly to sinking with crowds of ancestors sweating anxiously in dark woolen coats, trailing subcontinents & boiled potatoes & bitter little onions & radishes to set one's teeth on edge.

We found you in a basket on the doorstep.

We gambled you from the gypsies.

We raided the flickering region between worlds; in our haste to escape with you, we trod over countless other babies, leaving them stranded & gasping, but we never even gave them a second thought.

Reunion

It's the kind of encounter that's remembered for a lifetime—the twins separated at birth discovering each other on a cruise ship; the high school sweethearts who have neither laid eyes on nor heard tell of each other for thirty-one years, during which time each has married & been widowed (one of them, twice), running into each other at the base of the Washington Monument; the refugees of some long-lost fire, flood, war, or pestilence falling into each other's arms in the bus station of a town they are both merely passing through from separate departure points toward different destinations—complete with the ring of strangers gathering to feast on the embraces, the tears, the astonished cries: *But I thought you were dead—I couldn't see you in all the smoke, & then later, when no one knew where you were . . . !* or, *I wrote you so many times I lost count, but the letters always came back to me . . . !*

You won't be able to locate their sponsoring organization on the World Wide Web or in the Yellow Pages. It has no official designation, no mailing list. This is the group that stages "chance" reunions in public places for the sole purpose of engendering & inspiring hope in all who behold them. Clearly either the most cynical or the most altruistic society in the history of humankind, the group grows by a single person every time an onlooker in the crowd begins to suspect that all is not as it seems, & expresses doubt or even investigates, at which point, that individual is contacted & recruited. The alternative to signing up is on-the-spot execution.

Of course, the obvious problem with the group's "recruitment" strategy is that theoretically, if enough people catch on, everyone in the world would eventually become a member, thus defeating the organization's very purpose: if no one isn't in on it, who is there left to deceive?

But here's the genius of the set-up: nobody knows the identities of anyone else in the group, except for those of their own cell members!

So imagine teams of fake reuniters sent out amongst the populace, certain that the gathering crowd is taking everything at face value. It is for the sake of the bystanders that they feign the passion of reunion, & it is for the sake of the performers that the bystanders feign belief. Everyone is moved. Everyone goes home full of good feeling, unaware that they have deceived &/or been deceived.

It's simple, elegant, & entirely fool-proof, don't you agree? You must, of course. You are the final recruitee, the only one in the world who didn't know.

And now you do.

Convergence

Ms. Swenson, your party awaits you at the Information Desk. Ms. Swenson, your party awaits you at the Information Desk. As the intercom voice subsides into static, then silence, I wonder how long Ms. Swenson has been wandering in search of her party. At last, its location has been revealed to her! Her party has been roaming a long time, too, through Neolithic famines, through the Bronze Age, the Inquisition, the Plagues, the Wars of the Roses, etc., but now she's finally on her way to meet it, perhaps already stepping off the silver escalator. The bejeweled elephants shake their heads so that the bells on their fringed headpieces emit rusty chimes, & the aged hostess in her spangled, spaghetti-strapped tutu struggles to prop up the cake. It doesn't matter how late you are; if it's truly your party, you can trust it to wait for you.

Desiccation

The way she'd remembered it, Lot's wife had been transformed into a *pillow*, not a *pillar*, of salt, which made perfect sense, since hadn't Jacob used a stone for a headrest? Like the habits of extremophiles, those organisms she'd learned about on the Discovery Channel which thrive only in volcanic fire or arctic ice, no doubt the Biblical customs were perfectly suited to the weird, harsh desert environment that clearly necessitated such innovations. Being turned into salt was probably not all that different from the process she'd seen advertised on TV infomercials for LifeGem, the company that compacts the crematorium ashes of the beloved dead into flawless, polished diamonds, either a large single gem or a cluster of tasteful baguettes. How handy this must have been for Lot, who, rather than arranging for a funeral, would simply have hoisted the vaguely female-shaped block of salt onto his donkey's back. At night, under the blazing lattice of the oriental sky, he'd press his cheek against her, not even needing to weep, since she had already crystallized into all the tears any couple might ever require. And if he was sparing, little pinches of her flesh crumbled between his finger & thumb would provide savor for his stew throughout the rest of his life, like salty stars sizzling on his taste-buds, cauterizing the lining of his throat.

Sugar Constellation

High in the eastern sky, a girl isn't following instructions.
Instead of jumping out of the cake, she's descending into it.

At first, of course, the guys clustered dimly in her vicinity assume it's some
    kind of tease.
The most inebriated one attempts to clamber down after her,
but the icing refuses him entry, exactly the opposite of quicksand.

Like witnesses of an accidental drowning, they don't figure out until it's
    too late
that she's not coming back up.

The fact that they are equally enraged at & terrified of the cake
renders them incapable of moving away from it, so there they still hover,
cloudy & confused.

Meanwhile, the girl tip-tapping in her high heels down the caramelized
    sugar staircase
realizes that she can't even remember the last time she's been alone.

Has she become doll-size, or has the cake expanded around her?

It doesn't matter; here she can stretch out her arms in all directions
without brushing against the fragrant, spongy walls.

Now she will become a sucronaut,
the galaxy's first cartographer of the powdery abyssal zones,

then move on to map other events & entities
that are larger on the inside than they are on the outside:

the boredom of children; the anticipation of falling;
the molten landscape of a woodstove; an iceberg's amnesia;

the tenebrous heart of the musk rose; the eye of a microsuturing needle;
the silver queen bee of the subspecies *apis furiosa*.

Passage

1.

Sluiced down the drain in a gush of hot water, the diamond ring chimes delightedly against the sides of the pipe, no longer doomed to subsist as that stranger's lapidary appeasement.

Beneath her lurks an apparently endless involution of pipes, ducts, flumes, clogged chambers, plugged apertures, swollen bubbles of slime wherein her sidereal nature might be forever snared.

In such circumstances, it is an advantage to be narrow, dense, vastly polished, & not particularly polite.

Declining to tarry with anyone she meets, either in the coils of the city's waterworks, or, decades later, in the crosscuts, shafts, & airways of the earth itself, she snubs fossilized tortoise shells glowing like leather saddles; flames wandering lost without their wicks; the left pinky bone of the shipwrecked orphan mothered by a flock of glaciers; & everything else that has found its way in through wells, grates & manholes, through sinkholes, ponds, & steaming fissures, until she taps at last on the iron roof of the nethermost room in the world, where she must burn forever to be taken in.

2.

It isn't an act of rejection when the earth releases the wounded plough head; the Viking sail preserved in peat; the true Cardiff giant rising face up a half-inch a century through layers of soil, as if reluctantly surfacing from a bath, not even a mile from the spot where the false one was planted.

Hasn't each known its season of tumbling through mica-spangled waves: the molds to scour, the loams to cleanse?

That which has been covered must now be given back to shocks of wakefulness & pangs of air.

II.

Sidekick

She fell in love with the retired man next door when she heard that he spent several hours each week visiting his sidekick.

No doubt his sidekick had suffered a serious injury during one of their escapades, & now, permanently disabled, resided with others of his rank in an extended care facility, a pleasant building on one of the town's older avenues, where each of the sidekicks would have long since staked out a favorite spot on the spacious, screened-in porch or under one of the spreading elms to sit in a wheelchair, sip iced tea, & wait for visitors—a superhero, an arch-nemesis, anyone. But alas, Batman wouldn't show up except for on the occasional Christmas Eve when he'd stumble in disheveled & intoxicated, & the Green Lantern & Aquaman wouldn't even bother to send birthday cards. Only her sweetheart would arrive punctually at 2 P.M. every Saturday afternoon, tapping along the flagstone walkway with his rubber-tipped bamboo cane.

But it wasn't long before she dumped him, all the magic having evaporated for her the instant she replaced the battery in her hearing aid & discovered that he'd merely been visiting his *psychic*.

Versions of Cecily

According to the cultural elite

Cecily was a performance artist who combined the folky quaintness of "naive" or "primitive" art with the hypertheatrical exhibitionism of the urban "happening." People traveled from all over to gape at her, & her "act" was filmed by two documentary artists, one who interwove a background score of dulcimer music, & the other who, funded by an unusually sizeable Arts Council grant, commissioned Philip Glass to compose a meditation with oboe & titanium slide.

According to contemporary medical consensus

Cecily suffered from a chemical imbalance causing severe obsessive-compulsive behavior in the form of a series of bizarre, self-reinforcing aversive or "warding-off" rituals. She was featured in *Ripley's Believe It Or Not!* & the highly prestigious *OCD Chronicle,* Vol. 45, Issue 20, Section III, pp. 70–81, with 16.9 footnotes.

According to her neighbors & kin

Cecily was neither a visionary nor a victim, but merely a paragon of practicality, an example to point out to one's daughters.

How it began

One day some thirty years ago, when Cecily was sitting on her front step drying her ankle-length hair in the sunshine, her neighbor's son, distracted by the sight of that lustrous flow of honey & amber, tripped over a stump, dropping his basket of eggs & breaking every one. Crouched hissing & spitting over the shattered shells & oozing yolks, his mother raged, *A curse be on your hair! By the time the last curl dries, you shall be forever blind!*

Well, now, that's that

thought Cecily with relief. She'd been expecting a hex ever since she'd begun to blossom & glow at the age of twelve, & it might have turned out to be so much more baneful than this one, which was clearly workable. That she hadn't been cursed with a hog's snout or a crow's voice she attributed to the fact that it was still early, so the neighbor woman, though venomous as ever, was not as alert as she would be in an hour or so, & thus had not invested any serious consideration in her curse before she'd used it up.

She possessed only a one-spell-per-individual kind of power, so after she'd aimed it at you, you always knew from then on exactly where you stood.

Lingering on the front step for another moment or two

Cecily enjoyed the sensation of heavy dampness against the back of her neck. Then she rose to her feet, stretched, & disappeared in the shadowy coolness of the house, returning a minute later with a china teacup bordered with gilt cherry blossoms & filled with water. She settled herself back down on the step, dipped a strand of hair into the cup, & began to plan.

The first decades

were all about water. These were the years of experimentation with the saturation point of hair at different times of day & in different seasons, with fluid mechanics & various hydraulic systems including battery-powered tiny fountains, flumes, sluices, pressure nozzles, funnels, & steam generators artfully fastened into her hair with clasps, pins, trusses, hairnets constructed from fiberglass & tulle, & bejewelled, wicked-looking tiaras. One of the documentary films shows her with an enormous, teased beehive into which she'd inserted miniature slides for little handmade plasticine dolls to slide down; to the delight of neighborhood children, every Fourth of July she'd turn herself into a walking water park complete with a little whirlpool. For all her efficiency, however, there was a certain pulpiness about her presence. In her vicinity, the relative humidity was always extremely high. When she went grocery shopping in town, she'd stride through Wal Mart inside a veil of fine mist. People still joke about combing her hair for kelp. *A River Ran Through Her,* they say.

Later, growing bored with her own accomplishments

she began to work with mosses & soils, packing her scalp with various damp loams & silts. For a long time, it appeared as if she had donned a huge, misshapen helmet; her skull was so deep in peat that *The Weekly World News* claimed a shrunken Viking had been found preserved in her curls. She also acquired a nearly nautical expertise with all kinds of knots, braids, & coils in order to retain moisture. You didn't see her much about town during that era, but when she did venture out, her head was heavy but unbowed.

When the drought came & stayed

all day long, the hens roasted in their coops; when the sun went down, you could slice them open & scoop out the hard boiled eggs. Ears of corn spontaneously combusted inside their husks, as if the fields had been invaded by a camouflaged legion of paparazzi whose cameras continuously flashed. At the summer revivals, instead of going to the river, the elders had to dig graves & cover the new converts with dirt for them to rise up out of in their white gowns, but before the preacher could croak out the baptizing words, he had to bite into the flesh of his own wrist to wet his lips with blood. Downtown, the friction of high heels on sidewalks set off sparks. In the bar, each shot glass of whiskey bore its own little cloud of flame. Even the statues in the Cathedral of St. Lachrymosa of the Everlasting Condolences ceased to weep. When it came time for the "Symphony in the Park Festival," tuxedo'd firefighters positioned themselves next to the string section to spray the instruments with foam every time the bow action set them ablaze. No one ever looked up lest they behold the chalky bones of the sky beginning to crumble into powder to descend relentlessly upon them, caking their skin & hair, & collapsing their roofs & bridges. No one dared look down, either, lest they see that the earth's skin was cracking open to reveal the three tongues of Cerberus lolling pathetically out toward where the River Styx used to flow.

With water rationing so severely enforced

everybody wondered what Cecily would do. Bets were placed, stakes were circulated. That's when she ventured into alternate fluids, including common household liquids such as moonshine, & olive oil, & more glamorous ones such as heliotrope perfume & crème de menthe. She also experimented with unguents & gels including paraffin, glycerine, & various cosmetic creams & dentifrices. Some folks grumbled that she was cheating, since the clear implication of the original hex concerned water only. Cecily's admirers, on the other hand, maintained that her hair was not, in fact, dry, & wasn't that the point?

Eventually, it began to rain.

The drought came to an end, but Cecily did not return to her soil phase or her water park phase. She simply stayed outside a lot, letting the rain pour down on her. She was middle-aged now, & people speculated that she was changing, turning some kind of corner. Shunning the fabulous displays of the early years, she had entered what would turn out to be an extended minimalist period, which she has yet to leave. She keeps a clipped curl inside a mostly full bottle of tap water in the freezer, thus ensuring that some part of her hair will never dry, & sports a short, professional style that requires almost no tinkering on her part. She works as an accountant, & her services are highly in demand, since she can locate or even create a loophole for anyone. She's the most matter-of-fact person you'd ever hope to meet. The cultural elite speculate that she has "re-visioned," even redefined her work in terms of subterfuge & understatement. The medical establishment theorizes that her brain has finally begun to manufacture its own seratonin. Her friends & family agree that, like most women her age, she has merely figured out the simplest way to get around the system.

But some people say

that if you can get her to laugh, you might glimpse a strand of hair, part amber, part gray, taped to the underside of her tongue.

Gold

1. Boutique

Unable to choose between one hundred identical skinny little dresses of pure punishment gold, she stands there to this day, her gold kid-leather stiletto ankle boots sending ever-deeper scorch marks into the Turkish carpet.

2. Remnant

What to do with this one-inch square of sheer gold wrapping paper, too heavy to be cut into a fingernail-size funnel kite to soar from a human hair in the rising wind of a charcoal brazier, but too light to wrap around the last family heirloom, a frozen wedge of white butter stamped with the severe profile of Queen Victoria?

3. Phototherapeutic

Stretched out naked in the neonatal unit, his eyes shielded from the lights by a strip of black cloth, the infant resembles a large-ish Sultana raisin or an elderly bald pirate sunbathing on a nude beach in the Riviera. The pediatrician claims it's a high level of bilirubin in the bloodstream that tints his eyes & skin yellow, but the mother begs to differ. All winter, she's gone coatless, aglow amidst ice storms & freezing gusts; why shouldn't her lit womb have produced a golden child?

4. Vegetal

Squash is gold. Certain varieties of greenhouse-grown polar tomatoes are gold. In moonlight, albino carrots burn a steady low-voltage gold. But most savory are those vegetables whose hidden gold must be coaxed—or, as vegetable advocates insist, tortured—out of them by the application of heat. Consider, for example, the Vidalia onion. Sliced into a glass pan, laved in clear olive oil, & set upon a medium flame, it immediately shrivels as if from shock, then expands into translucence under your gaze, releasing a rarified golden blush which its reticent nature has hitherto hidden even from itself.

5. Inconsolable

He weeps because he can no longer scrape from slab walls that spongy golden fungus whose delicate bitterness so strangely satisfied his thirst. Upon his release from prison, he smuggled out several strips, stuffing them between his raw ankles & his pitiful socks, but in the open air of the wider world, it withered & soon crumbled, despite the fact that to the extreme discomfiture of his (by now) elderly wife & grown children, he spared no effort in attempting to recreate in his home the exact varieties of dankness & darkness that oppressed him these last twenty-nine years.

6. Family Secret

Passed down from mother to daughter through generations, the process reputedly has something to do with phlogiston, with naphthalene, with oil of angelica & attar of jasmine, with reagents, desiccators, & sulfate paper, but no one knows for sure. The resulting phenomenon has been photographed since the late 1860s, when it was first captured on daguerreotype: a single print remains of the seated bride suffering the prolonged immobility required for her wedding portrait. Her gown, a whalebone-corseted, cincture-bodiced, pearl-buttoned, high-collared contraption, seems more severe than elegant. Her gaze is steady, only barely discernibly bored. The scene's only vibrance appears in the radiance flowing around the sausage-curl-&-ringlet sculpture of her hair—her wedding veil, you assume at first, but even in this overexposed, dimensionlessly bright print, you can tell that there's something odd about the way it fans out, the structure of its line & weave. After a moment, you realize with a shock that it's nothing less than a bridal crown of flame: her hair burns, but is not consumed.

Nowadays, of course, photographers can manipulate the darkness & density of surrounding shadows by adjusting the film speed setting, or they can reduce the amount of glare by increasing their actual distance from the subject while zooming in; thus, the flames show up distinctly in the modern glossy prints, each nimbused bride slicing the cake, hurling the bouquet, & dancing at arm's length with her groom, who must maintain a safe distance throughout the festivities.

Nevertheless, most people prefer the original daguerrotype, not despite but *because* of its weird, washed-out flatness, which seems to preserve the mystery of the phenomenon in a way that contemporary photography, forever associated in the public's mind with special effects & digital intervention, is unable to accomplish. In the imagination, that first print's flame burns ever a deeper gold beneath its sepia wash.

Chthonic

Dispatched centuries ago by some long-forgotten monarch to determine
the precise percentage of the underworld that was currently burning,
& to create a reliable atlas thereof,

the terranauts surfaced in the middle of a local baseball game in Mount
Vernon, Ohio at 8:41 on a slightly chilly April evening,

bursting through the sod to crouch blinking & shivering in the
hallucinatory effulgence of the vapor lamps, arguing in guttural
sputterings & hissings in their dead language over whether they had
broken out of the earth's crust someplace in the Occidental regions,
where it was noon at midnight & vice versa; or whether they had
surprised the Western sun in partial eclipse;

or whether perhaps they had not emerged from the earth at all, but had
merely stumbled upon some heretofore uncharted stratum of the
abyssal territories, & these were its denizens, serfs clad in the
mandatory uniform of whatever collective chastisement they were
enduring—

in fact, one of them even suffered the complete encagement of his face in
some kind of hideous wire mesh fused onto his head, & the mouths
of several of them spewed a noxious black stream of that strange
grit which was, no doubt, their enforced & only nourishment—

yes, this must be the explanation, & now the travelers must seek some
way to appease these vassals' trained tormenters who would
certainly be enraged at the interruption of their cruel sport,

& then they must chisel, chip, & tunnel their way upward through this
dusty undersky whose false lights so maliciously mimicked the
actual heavens of the outerworld where their king waited to be
informed of everything they had witnessed during their wanderings:

the subterranean waterfalls of molten glass; the sunken swamps aglow
with blue bacterial flame; the steaming chlorine lake they had named
"Alba Rosa" for its pale, bubbling efflorescences resembling hugely
misshapen blossoms; the crumbling passageways illumined by the
salt statues of saints, trolls, & princesses; the grottoes filled with the
skeletons of the victims of consumption who, after wintering on

their roofs in the overlands in hopes that the icy air would scour their
  lungs, had descended to seek healing in the caverns' mineral mists—
  candles below, constellations above, unless it was the other way
  around; the legions of slaves chained together at the ankles as they
  mined the heaving, blistering depths for zeroes (a difficult &
  dangerous work in which death by scalding was the rule rather than
  the exception) so that the overworld's supply of naughts & ciphers
  might continually be refreshed—

oh, how to determine what percentage of the underworld was ablaze when
  so much of it was, or had recently been, or regretted not being, or was
  about to be again, so that it was impossible to distinguish between
  memories of flame & ambitions of conflagration?—

what kind of an atlas could they create when the territory was continually
  shifting from the inside out?—no, maps, they had decided, were for
  surfaces, not depths; they could no more draw up internal boundaries
  for this kingdom than they could for their own bellies—

their only hope was to present the king with concocted statistics & a
  fabricated map; he was, after all, infirm & gullible—what could he do
  but believe them,

& if he *didn't* believe them, he would have to go to the trouble of
  commissioning a second team for verification, & then another team
  after that, & another, & another,

so that eventually, everyone in the whole country would pass through the
  channels & cross the charred plains of Hades to arrive at last in this
  flat dirt field, oddly cool between layers of fire,

gazing at these suffering mortals with their terrible punishment gloves &
  face-cages, positioned quietly in small clusters or alone, as if there was
  no place in their world they'd rather stand.

Restraint

The day the furniture returned
of its own accord,
no one was peering out the window;
no one was scanning the horizon;
no one was walking by the cliffs
to gaze yearningly out to sea.
Instead, everyone was carrying on
as efficiently as possible
under the circumstances.
So when the sofa slipped quietly
into position under the window,
somehow we knew
not to exclaim.
When the cupboard edged its way
into the alcove,
we wisely pretended
not to notice.
When the dining room set gleamingly appeared,
we were careful
to avert our eyes.
It was like a scene by Henry James,
all nuances & sensibilities
richly unexpressed.
When supper time arrived,
we simply sat down
as if nothing had ever been
any different.
Neither affecting too high a level of decorum
nor betraying too deep a feeling of relief,
we lifted our long-lost forks,
& began to eat.

Majesty

Exclaiming, *At last, I am Queen!* she commissioned a team of one thousand spelunkers, surveyors, meteorologists, pastry chefs, Abstract Expressionists, cartographers, gynecologists, seismeticians, & ecclesiasts to determine whether or not the darkest hour actually occurs just before the dawn.

As well as encumbering her operatives with the most state-of-the-art instruments of their respective fields, she also equipped them with old-time walkie-talkies. How she adored the static, the squawking, the wacky handles they concocted for each other!

All night, every night, she'd perch on her throne, munching rampion (which, she'd been told, queens fancy), & eavesdropping as they discussed the color, flavor, density, texture, adhesiveness, etc. of various strata of darkness—over here at 1 A.M., thickening, but still a little runny, more like tar than like velvet, over there at 3:00, hardening into obsidian, but still slightly soft at the center.

Specialist

She thought, *But am I not far too old for a whole new field?*

Having invented her own Ph.D. program at Oxford by combining credits from the disciplines of Linguistics, Mechanical Physics, Audiology, Operatic History, & Tonal Dysphoria, & thus emerging as the world's only Doctor of Human Subverbal Utterances,

she had, throughout the past four decades, become renowned throughout the world as the Margaret Mead of that vast culture of mutterers, hummers, groaners, growlers, wailers, whimperers, weepers, grunters, chokers, coughers, belchers, stutterers, splutterers, susurraters, screamers, screechers, sniggerers, gigglers, yodelers, bellowers, snorers, chucklers, idioglossics, ululators, & dysphrasics to which we all, at varying frequencies, belong.

Yet now as the flames of her sixtieth birthday candles sputtered out under the little local gale of her expelled breath, she understood that she had been inexcusably lazy, halting precisely when she should have gone on, *beyond* the subverbal all the way into the subvocal—those beautiful, uncharted realms of gasping, sighing, spitting, clicking, snuffling, whispering, hissing, wheezing, lipsmacking, toothsucking, mouthing, miming, & whistling.

Only for an instant did she hesitate before she pushed back her chair & departed at once for the airport, never to be heard from again.

Some claim that she perished in a lava flow while seeking a pyrophoric environment where even the lightest exhalation would either liquefy into flames or balloon out into the glistening transparency of blown glass; others contend that she succumbed to hypothermia in Verkhoyansk, where a single breath freezes instantly as it leaves the soft warm cave of the mouth, then drops to the tundra at an as-yet-uncalibrated rate of speed, shattering almost inaudibly.

Balneology

It's true that the body longs to be submerged, but its separate parts also clamor for their own individual immersions.

The head will create any excuse, such as a craving for Popsicles, in order to savor the icy mists of the freezer, even though it knows that the last Popsicle has been melded mushily to the package of green beans for months.

Nothing is more delectable to the eyes than the darkness bath, which is why they are constantly blinking. Any tincture of heart-brine in the form of humiliating, held-back tears only heightens the experience.

The tongue lives for aftertaste—not the glycerin bath of melting marzipan, but the creamy surge left behind.

The arm longs to be extended through the window of a moving car into the rain, a double bath of water & ozone wind. On such occasions, the arm often finds itself waving foolishly in time to the radio music, as if it belongs to a famous conductor whom everyone addresses as "Maestro."

The fingers enjoy· many kinds of baths, such as wax, dough, & sand. Recently, a woman was apprehended at the Natural Bridge, Virginia gift shop for plunging her hands deep into the bucket of polished bits of amethyst, carnelian, leopard jasper, hematite, rose quartz, snowflake obsidian, & lace agate.

No, not for plunging them in, but for refusing to remove them.

To the Atlantic Ocean

For decades I neglected to pet & comb you.
Though others did not cease to lean over you
with their cutlery & coaxing susurrations,
I neither smoothed your bed nor tended your plumy borders;
I never tested the mist of your breath on my little silver-backed mirror;
& on the one occasion when silk stockings entered my life
with birds-of-paradise vermillioning up the thighs,
I kept them for myself, though others no doubt would have traveled
   via Greyhound all the way from the west coast, guarding them
   triply-wrapped on their laps in order to offer them, sobbing,
   to you.

Nevertheless,
when I rounded that corner yesterday in Belmar, N.J.,
there you were with your swellings & lassitudes, your flocks & panoplies,
no less voluminous for me
than for anyone else present.

Shade

If she hadn't been raised in English fog, then transplanted to Seattle mist at the age of twelve, tiptoeing around her mother's migraines in heavily-curtained rooms on both continents;

if she hadn't attended Appalachian Central College, overshadowed by rock & set about with pine;

if she hadn't majored in film history, spending both undergraduate & graduate years with ancient, fragile reels in dim lecture halls;

if she hadn't married a speleologist & spent most of her daylight adult life with him beneath the earth's surface;

if her thick, dark, curly hair hadn't been forever springing about her face, so that you could scarcely glimpse her eyes;

if she hadn't suffered from a permanent crick in her neck due to all that poring over old celluloid & ducking under stalactites, so that her head was always slightly bent;

if, despite the Surgeon General's warning, she hadn't been a heavy smoker, so that she was perpetually wreathed in blue cumuli;

if she hadn't been told by many people that she looked fabulous in hats, which, in fact, she did;

then perhaps it would not have taken her until she was fifty-one years old to discover that just as the silkworm secretes silk thread, & the squid exudes its murky cloud,

she possessed the power of emitting darkness through the pores of her skin, radiating deep shade & a five-degree temperature drop from her body in a local penumbra of one-&-a-half feet, an ability she deemed both uninteresting & impractical, & therefore did not mention to anyone ever.

When she dies, her unspent shade will remain coiled within her under her coffin lid, unless, of course, she is cremated, in which case it will be scattered with her ashes at one of the sites she found meaningful in life—foggy Britain, misty Seattle, densely-wooded Appalachia, or those deep caverns where visitors can experience that ultimate obscurity known as "total cave darkness."

Initiate

That wave hurtling along
at the speed of its own homelessness
is frantically searching its memory
for information that might help it survive
intact, but because it finds nothing except a habit
of smoothness, a long-term acquaintance
with the sky (that placid, parallel existence
clearly about to be disrupted),
the wave concludes that this must be
its very first time.
It resolves for the sake of its tribe
to be brave, even though it's nothing
but a quivering heap of bubbles
competing with each other to be
smallest, propelled in loops back & forth
as it tries vainly to unclench itself
within a space so narrow
& at a pace so languid
it has time to compose
an original song entitled
I Am a Pilgrim & a Stranger
just before it overbalances, crests,
& breaks at the precise instant when,
pondering whether it would be more terrifying
to imagine oneself as helpless,
propelled by forces utterly beyond control,
or as glaringly bright,
a wall of muscled glory
descending upon a quaking world,
it concludes that the answer is
yes.

Extrospection

Because of everything we desire & therefore project,
& everything we dread & therefore hallucinate;

because of what used to be present, but is present no longer,
though everyone yet navigates around it,
& what is not present now, but might one day become so,
though it already exerts gravity,
casting shadows that shoulder other shadows aside—

because of this crowd, one might assume
there wouldn't be much room left
for anything else at all;

but if you herded onto the drive-in movie screen of the sky
everyone's phantasms, figments, eidolons, mirages, & chimera,

together, they would form merely
a kind of languidly teeming smudge right there above the horizon,
not precisely at two o'clock, but just a little to the left,
depending on where you stand.

Work

It is nothing but labor to occupy the ocean.
The body requests permission to rest,
but rest is not granted.
The arms go round & round without ceasing;
the legs pump back & forth;
the head turns from side to side for air & light,
everything striving against undertow.

The mind, too, travails.
It wants to create metaphors about buoyancy & flow;
it wants to delineate the clouds foaming above;
it wants to quote Matthew Arnold:
Now the great winds shoreward blow,
Now the salt tides seaward flow,
blah blah blah.

The birds, as well, are industrious, diving & calling;
& the light is just barely on schedule
in its task of polishing the waves;
& the sea itself is famous for never resting.
That is its work: the churning & roaring,
the seething & slapping,
the inexhaustible rising up
& the relentless hurling down.

Yet just as in deep forest,
the tiny, multitudinous notchings & serrations,
the leafy inspikings & upturnings
comprise the larger smoothness that is moss,
& we say,
When they grew too weary to continue on their way,
the children laid their heads on pillows of moss,

so these kickings & strokings,
these whirlings & strainings,
this continuous exchange of transfer & refusal—
all these together become
that particular kind of rest
one must fight to enter
& flail against to leave.

Bridge Escort

I suspect it's not falling that people fear, it's rising into a blue that breaks open
   without mercy & without anesthesia.
I've been tempted to blindfold them, like horses led from a blazing barn.
I've been tempted to smack them,
or to open the door & push them out, abandoning them right in the
   middle.
But I don't really blame them.
It's eerie, crossing over, & the bridge sings & sways in the cross-winds.
All bridges hate stillness, long to break loose,
though it's the secret ones that get to me,
the microspans between twilight & dusk; remorse & regret; slate & ash—
the smaller they are, the worse they vibrate & hum.
Vertigo or rapture of the deep:
it's enough to bring you to your knees a hundred times a day;
I was raised Baptist, but I'm an Incrementalist now;
sometimes when I close my eyes I can feel the Holy Ghost
opening ever-narrower spaces for me to get lost in.
That's when I remind myself of those rare riders
who fall asleep in my truck like babies in car seats—
they lean their heads back, & they're out.
When I stop at the other side,
I like to watch them for a moment before I wake them;
I like to imagine them connecting the stars inside their bodies
or wandering through their childhood homes, amazed to find everything
so much larger than they'd remembered.

To A Sky

Do you remember just now
when you were a baby,
not all-the-way unscrolled from your birth caul
blue as bludgeoned silk?
You couldn't yet distinguish
between *inside* & *outside,*
between reflections & their shadows,
between the voice crying in the wilderness
& the wilderness wandering inside the voice.
It was far too early
for adjectives or for Andromeda,
& you weren't ready,
would never be ready,
for sedimentary cloudburn
porous as angelskin coral;
for the glow that smolders
between bandage & wound;
for the luminous, histrionic claustrophobia of snow globes;
or the amnesia that spreads like a radioactive stain
across a fever's surface.
You would never be ready for ice light
or the night-blooming cereus
polllinated by tipsy moths;
for the rain before the rain;
for the silver boiling over at the heart of a wave.
Moist & raw,
you were far too young to ponder
that single gasp you took
before you were flung out,
released & plummeting.
You didn't know how to float,
& you didn't know how to fly;
swimming wouldn't be invented for millennia;
& you couldn't find
a flaw or a crack or a snag
to slow you down
or give you refuge—
so without either precedent or permission,
the only thing you could do
was to open.

Acknowledgments

These poems (some in earlier versions) appeared in the following publications:

DIAGRAM: "Leap"

Melic Review: "Extrospection"

Ninth Letter: "Bridge Escort," "To a Sky"

Third Coast: "Initiate"

Triquarterly: "Gold," "Sisters," "The Top 21 Holiday, Party, & Everyday Stains, & How to Remove Them"

"Leap" also appeared in *DIAGRAM: Selections from the Magazine,* ed. Ander Monson, del Sol Press, 2003.

Many thanks are due to Mark Halliday, David Dodd Lee, Rick Mulkey, & Herb Scott for generous editorial assistance.

photo by Jon Bateman

Claire Bateman is the author of four other collections of poetry: *The Bicycle Slow Race* (1991), *Friction* (1998), *At the Funeral of the Ether* (1998), and *Clumsy* (2003). She has won the Louisiana Literature Poetry Prize, the New Millennium Writing Prize, a Tennessee Arts Commission Literary Award, a National Endowment for the Arts Poetry Fellowship, a Robert Frost Fellowship, a Writing Teacher Portfolio Award from Scholastic Arts, and most recently, a Pushcart Prize. She teaches at the Fine Arts Center in Greenville, South Carolina.

New Issues Poetry & Prose

Editor, Herbert Scott

Vito Aiuto, *Self-Portrait as Jerry Quarry*
James Armstrong, *Monument in a Summer Hat*
Claire Bateman, *Clumsy, Leap*
Maria Beig, *Hermine: An Animal Life* (fiction)
Kevin Boyle, *A Home for Wayward Girls*
Michael Burkard, *Pennsylvania Collection Agency*
Christopher Bursk, *Ovid at Fifteen*
Anthony Butts, *Fifth Season, Little Low Heaven*
Kevin Cantwell, *Something Black in the Green Part of Your Eye*
Gladys Cardiff, *A Bare Unpainted Table*
Kevin Clark, *In the Evening of No Warning*
Cynie Cory, *American Girl*
Peter Covino, *Cut Off the Ears of Winter*
Jim Daniels, *Night with Drive-By Shooting Stars*
Darren DeFrain, *The Salt Palace* (fiction)
Joseph Featherstone, *Brace's Cove*
Lisa Fishman, *The Deep Heart's Core Is a Suitcase*
Robert Grunst, *The Smallest Bird in North America*
Paul Guest, *The Resurrection of the Body and the Ruin of the World*
Robert Haight, *Emergences and Spinner Falls*
Mark Halperin, *Time as Distance*
Myronn Hardy, *Approaching the Center*
Brian Henry, *Graft*
Edward Haworth Hoeppner, *Rain Through High Windows*
Cynthia Hogue, *Flux*
Christine Hume, *Alaskaphrenia*
Janet Kauffman, *Rot* (fiction)
Josie Kearns, *New Numbers*
David Keplinger, *The Clearing*
Maurice Kilwein Guevara, *Autobiography of So-and-So: Poems in Prose*
Ruth Ellen Kocher, *When the Moon Knows You're Wandering, One Girl Babylon*
Gerry LaFemina, *The Window Facing Winter*
Steve Langan, *Freezing*
Lance Larsen, *Erasable Walls*
David Dodd Lee, *Abrupt Rural, Downsides of Fish Culture*
M.L. Liebler, *The Moon a Box*
Deanne Lundin, *The Ginseng Hunter's Notebook*
Barbara Maloutas, *In a Combination of Practices*
Joy Manesiotis, *They Sing to Her Bones*

Sarah Mangold, *Household Mechanics*
Gail Martin, *The Hourglass Heart*
David Marlatt, *A Hog Slaughtering Woman*
Louise Mathias, *Lark Apprentice*
Gretchen Mattox, *Buddha Box, Goodnight Architecture*
Paula McLain, *Less of Her; Stumble, Gorgeous*
Lydia Melvin, *South of Here*
Sarah Messer, *Bandit Letters*
Malena Mörling, *Ocean Avenue*
Julie Moulds, *The Woman with a Cubed Head*
Gerald Murnane, *The Plains* (fiction)
Marsha de la O, *Black Hope*
C. Mikal Oness, *Water Becomes Bone*
Bradley Paul, *The Obvious*
Elizabeth Powell, *The Republic of Self*
Margaret Rabb, *Granite Dives*
Rebecca Reynolds, *Daughter of the Hangnail, The Bovine Two-Step*
Martha Rhodes, *Perfect Disappearance*
Beth Roberts, *Brief Moral History in Blue*
John Rybicki, *Traveling at High Speeds* (expanded second edition)
Mary Ann Samyn, *Inside the Yellow Dress, Purr*
Ever Saskya, *The Porch is a Journey Different From the House*
Mark Scott, *Tactile Values*
Hugh Seidman, *Somebody Stand Up and Sing*
Martha Serpas, *Côte Blanche*
Diane Seuss-Brakeman, *It Blows You Hollow*
Elaine Sexton, *Sleuth*
Marc Sheehan, *Greatest Hits*
Sarah Jane Smith, *No Thanks—and Other Stories* (fiction)
Heidi Lynn Staples, *Guess Can Gallop*
Phillip Sterling, *Mutual Shores*
Angela Sorby, *Distance Learning*
Matthew Thorburn, *Subject to Change*
Russell Thorburn, *Approximate Desire*
Rodney Torreson, *A Breathable Light*
Robert VanderMolen, *Breath*
Martin Walls, *Small Human Detail in Care of National Trust*
Patricia Jabbeh Wesley, *Before the Palm Could Bloom: Poems of Africa*